SCL
11/06

JAGUARS

A TRUE BOOK®

by
Ann O. Squire

Children's Press®
A Division of Scholastic Inc.

New York Toronto London Auckland Sydney
Mexico City New Delhi Hong Kong
Danbury, Connecticut

A jaguar in Belize

Reading Consultant
Nanci R. Vargus, Ed.D.
Assistant Professor,
School of Education,
University of Indianapolis

Content Consultant
Kathy Carlstead, Ph.D.
Research Scientist,
Honolulu Zoo

Dedication:
For Emma

Library of Congress Cataloging-in-Publication Data

Squire, Ann.
    Jaguars / by Ann O. Squire.
        p. cm. — (A true book)
Includes bibliographical references and index.
    ISBN 0-516-22793-9 (lib. bdg.)   0-516-27933-5 (pbk.)
    1. Jaguar—Juvenile literature. I. Title. II. Series.
QL737.C23S6395 2004
599.75'5—dc22
                                                    2004007756

1 2 3 4 5 6 7 8 9 10 R 14 13 12 11 10 09 08 07 06 05

Contents

A jaguar creeping through a
rain forest in Central America

Cat of Mystery

Of all the world's wild cats, few are as mysterious as the jaguar. This beautiful cat has a spotted coat that looks a lot like that of a leopard. The jaguar is the largest cat in the Western Hemisphere. The Western Hemisphere is the half of the world that includes North, Central, and South America.

The jaguar's body is heavy and stocky. Its short, muscular legs are designed for swimming, climbing, and crawling. The jaguar has a large head and very strong jaws. These

Jaguars are stockier than most other big cats.

Jaguars are excellent climbers.

jaws allow the jaguar to crack open the hard shells of turtles and to bite through the skulls of **tapirs** and other **prey** animals.

For thousands of years, the people of Central and South America have feared and admired jaguars. Some even believed that these cats had special powers.

The Maya were an ancient **civilization** in Central America and Mexico. They believed that jaguars were a link between the world of the living and the world of the dead, and they worshipped a jaguar-god. To them, a jaguar's spotted coat represented the stars in the sky. The Maya also believed that Earth was flat with four corners. They thought that at each corner, a different-colored jaguar held up the sky.

The Olmec, another ancient people, believed in "were-jaguars." These were creatures that were half-human, half-jaguar. They

The Maya, Olmec, and Aztec peoples all believed that the jaguar had special powers. This Mayan jaguar throne (top), Aztec calender symbol (above left) and Olmec sculpture (above right) show the great respect these ancient peoples had for this mysterious cat.

thought that some people could transform themselves into jaguars.

To the Aztec, jaguars were a connection to the spirit world. To please the gods, the Aztec sometimes **sacrificed** humans and fed their hearts to these big cats.

If you travel to Mexico or Central America today, you can visit the ruins of many ancient cities. One of the most famous is the Mayan city

The Temple of the Jaguars at Chichén Itzá

of Chichén Itzá, in Mexico. Here you can see many carvings of jaguars. There is even a huge building called the Temple of the Jaguars.

A Powerful Hunter

The Mayan word for jaguar is *yaguar,* meaning "he who kills with one leap." The cat's scientific name is *Panthera onca,* which clearly refers to this cat's impressive claws. *Panthera* means "hunter" and *onca* means "hook" or "barb." The jaguar is, in fact, an expert hunter. Its body and

senses are perfectly **adapted**
for the life it leads.

The jaguar is very strong,
but it is not a fast runner.
Instead of chasing down its
prey, the jaguar walks noise-
lessly through the forest, on

the lookout for any animal, big or small. When it sees an animal that is close by, the jaguar pounces on it. Then it kills its victim with a bite to the head.

The jaguar's front legs and shoulders are very muscular,

A jaguar leaping

giving this cat the strength to capture and kill many kinds of animals, from turtles and armadillos to full-grown cattle. Extra-long hind legs help the jaguar to leap on its prey, and razor-sharp front claws help it to grab and hold its food with ease. When the claws are not in use, the jaguar can retract them, or pull them back, into its paws. That way, the claws don't get dull when the cat walks.

Jaguars can retract their claws when they are not using them.

Even the jaguar's spotted coat helps the jaguar to hunt successfully. As this big cat moves through the forest, its black spots blend in with the

This jaguar's spotted coat helps it blend in with its rain-forest surroundings.

shadows, so that the jaguar can get very close to its prey before pouncing.

Like other **predators,** the jaguar has excellent senses of hearing and vision. The jaguar hunts mostly at dawn and dusk, and its senses help it to find prey during times when there is not much light.

A jaguar may wait up in a tree for prey to walk below. Then the jaguar leaps down upon the animal.

A jaguar attacking a peccary

One of the most difficult animals to catch is the peccary, a piglike creature that travels in groups of fifty to a hundred animals. A group of peccaries could easily defend itself against a jaguar, or even trample the big cat to death. The jaguar has come up with a clever way to capture a peccary, however. It simply waits in a tree until a herd of peccaries passes underneath, then leaps down and attacks one. After making a kill, the jaguar quickly climbs back up the tree. When the peccaries leave, the cat comes down to enjoy its dinner.

Jaguar or Leopard?

Jaguar

A jaguar looks a lot like a leopard. Both cats have **tawny** coats covered with **rosettes** of black spots. But it's really not that difficult to tell jaguars and leopards apart. The jaguar's rosettes have one or two small dots in the middle. The leopard's do not. The jaguar also has a thicker body and a shorter tail than the leopard.

Leopard

Black jaguar

Black versions of both leopards and jaguars are common, and it's very difficult to tell one from the other. This isn't a problem in the wild, though, because jaguars and leopards live on different continents. Jaguars live in Central and South America, and leopards live in Africa and Asia.

Black leopard

Where Jaguars Live

Many years ago, jaguars ranged from Arizona and Texas in the north all the way down to Argentina. Today, because of hunting, loss of **habitat,** and other threats, jaguars are not nearly so widespread. Most of these big cats are found in South America's Amazon Basin.

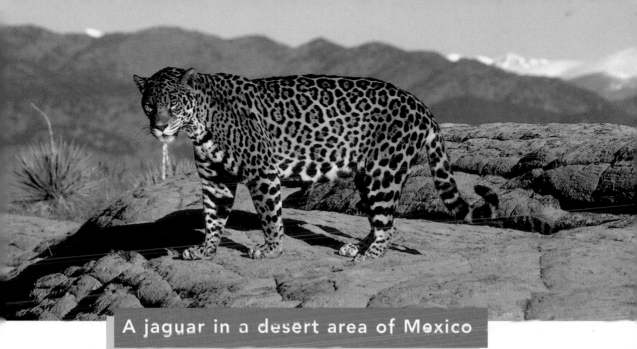

A jaguar in a desert area of Mexico

Unlike tigers, which live only in forests, jaguars do well in many kinds of habitats. They can adapt to tropical rain forests, swamps, grasslands, and deserts. They can even live in areas used by people for logging, ranching, and farming.

Unlike many other cats, jaguars like to be near water and are excellent swimmers.

One thing that most jaguar habitats have in common is a lake, river, stream, or other source of water. Jaguars are excellent swimmers and often eat fish and turtles.

Like almost all other cats, jaguars are solitary. They prefer to live by themselves rather than with other cats. They avoid one another by setting up territories where other jaguars are not welcome. In areas where there is plenty of food, a jaguar's territory can be very small. Where prey animals are hard to find, however, a territory may be a hundred times larger.

As a jaguar walks through its territory looking for food, it also marks the edges of the territory so that other cats

A jaguar marking its territory (left) and jaguars fighting over territory (below)

know the area is occupied. It may leave visual marks, such as scratches on a tree trunk, or smell markers, such as a spray of urine on a bush. Jaguars also roar **menacingly** to warn other jaguars to stay away.

A male jaguar's territory is usually much larger than that of a female. It is common for the territories of males and females to overlap. As we'll see in the next chapter, this comes in handy when it's time to find a mate.

Raising Cubs

One of the few times that jaguars get together is for mating. When a female jaguar is ready to find a mate, she walks around in her territory, and sometimes even moves outside it. Males looking for mates make mewing cries. Eventually, the

Male and female jaguars stay together only during mating time.

male and female find each other.

After mating, the male and female separate. About

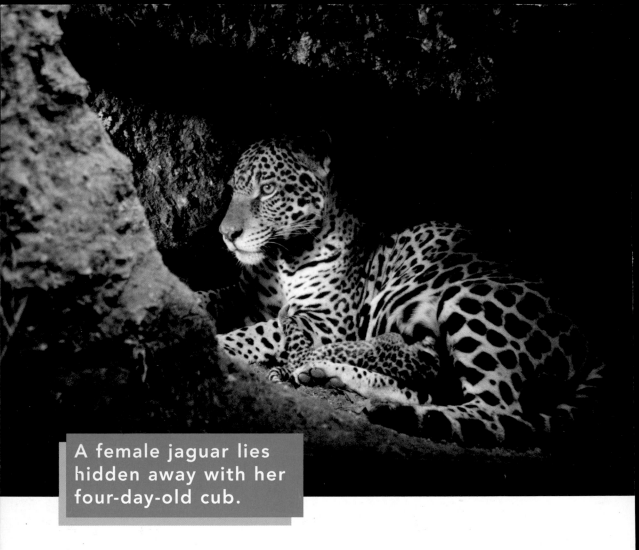

A female jaguar lies hidden away with her four-day-old cub.

three months later, the female makes a den in thick bushes or another protected place. There she gives birth to her cubs.

There are usually between one and four cubs in a litter, each weighing about 2 pounds (1 kilogram). The cubs are blind and helpless at first, but they grow very quickly.

A six-week-old jaguar cub

A jaguar mother and her part-grown cub near a pond in the rain forest

At about three months of age, they begin to go along with their mother when she goes hunting.

The cubs stay with their mother for nearly two years, learning everything they need to know to survive. Then they leave her and go off to estab-lish territories of their own.

In the wild, jaguars usually live between fifteen and twenty years. In zoos, they may reach twenty-five years of age.

Jaguars in Danger

Jaguars have no rivals in nature. No other wild animals hunt them. Since the jaguar is South America's top predator, you wouldn't expect it to be threatened by anything or anyone. Unfortunately, like many other wild cats around the world, jaguars have one very deadly enemy: humans.

This photograph shows humans clearing a part of Amazon Rain Forest in the South American country of Suriname. This area has long been home to jaguars.

As South America's popula-
tion grows, people move into
lands that once belonged to
jaguars. Forests are cut down
so the land can be used for
farms, towns, and cattle
ranches. With the forests
gone, jaguars have a hard
time finding enough to eat,
and they sometimes attack
cattle and other livestock.
When this happens, people
become angry and afraid. To

protect their animals and themselves, they trap, poison, or shoot jaguars.

Another problem is that in some areas where jaguars live, people like to hunt peccaries, tapirs, and deer. These are the same animals that jaguars eat. When there is not enough food to go around, jaguars usually lose.

Jaguars have long been hunted for their beautiful

Even though it is illegal, some people still hunt jaguars for their skins.

spotted coats, which are dis-played as hunting trophies or made into clothing. In the

1960s, as many as fifteen thousand jaguars were being killed every year in Brazil alone. In 1973, jaguars were declared an **endangered species,** and hunting these big cats became **illegal.** Although the number of jaguars killed each year has dropped, poaching, or illegal hunting, still goes on.

Even though jaguars are endangered, it's not too late to save them. **Conservation** organizations are working to set up protected areas where jaguars will be safe. They are trying to find ways to reduce the conflict between ranchers and jaguars. They are also trying to find other sources of food for people who hunt the same animals that jaguars do. With a little luck and lots of hard work, these beautiful spotted cats will roam the wild lands of South America for years to come.

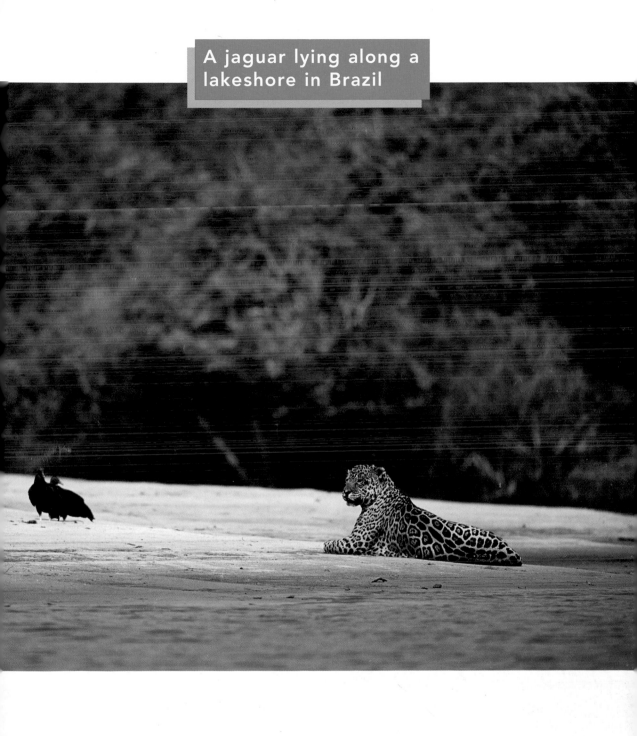

A jaguar lying along a lakeshore in Brazil

To Find Out More

Here are some additional resources to help you learn more about jaguars:

 **Books**

Lalley, Pat. **Jaguars** (Animals of the Rain Forest). Steck-Vaughn, 2000.

Malaspina, Ann. **The Jaguar** (Endangered Animals and Habitats). Lucent Books, 2000.

Stille, Darlene R. **Jaguars.** Compass Point Books, 2001.

Witt, Melanie. **Jaguars** (The Untamed World). Steck-Vaughn, 1998.

Woods, Theresa. **Jaguars** (Naturebooks). Child's World, 2001.

Organizations and Online Sites

The Belize Zoo—Jaguars
www.belizezoo.org/zoo/zoo/mammals/jag/jag1.html

At this Web site you can listen to the jaguar's roar.

Jaguar, Lord of the Mayan Jungle
http://www.oneworldjourneys.com/expeditions/jaguar/

Join a jaguar-tracking expedition in the Mexican jungle. Includes jaguar facts, photos, and film clips.

Save the Jaguar
www.savethejaguar.com

This Web site, sponsored by the Wildlife Conservation Society, gives a lot of information on jaguars, including threats to these animals and what is being done to save them.

Important Words

adapted changed over time to adjust to an environment

civilization highly organized society

conservation the act of protecting things in nature

endangered species groups of living things that are in danger of dying out

habitat place where a living thing naturally lives and grows

illegal against the law

menacingly threateningly

predators animals that hunt other animals

prey animal hunted by other animals

rosettes rose-shaped designs

sacrificed offered to God or a god

tapirs large mammals of Central and South America that have long snouts

tawny having a light, sandy-brown color

Index

Meet the Author

Ann O. Squire has a Ph.D. in animal behavior. Before becoming a writer, she spent several years studying African electric fish and the special signals they use to communicate with each other. Dr. Squire is the author of many books on animals and natural science topics, including *Leopards*, *Cheetahs*, *Tigers*, and *Lions*. She and her children, Emma and Evan, share their home with a not-so-wild cat named Isabel.